Book design and typography by Eloise Leigh
Typeset in Carter Sans Pro and Griffon
Printed in Germany by Umweltdruck Berlin GmbH

ISBN 979-8-9851704-1-2

DARK ENTRIES EDITIONS
910 Larkin Street, San Francisco, CA 94109
www.darkentriesrecords.com

THE
ARCHAEOLOGY
OF
EROS

POETRY BY
JORGE SOCARRAS

ART BY
MEL ODOM

DARK ENTRIES
EDITIONS

ON THE ARCHAEOLOGY OF EROS

Romantic feelings can sweep us away, make us feel powerless, lift us to new heights. Especially overwhelming when we are young, they can without warning make us feel as young again at any point in life. As a young man I started writing poems as a way of probing the mystery of these feelings, attempting to articulate the experience of attraction and longing, crystalize something in essence intangible. Often these were paeans to those who prompted such feelings—other men mostly, but with exceptions. (Beauty transcends gender!) Poems were also a way of honoring the feelings themselves. Because romantic feeling does not always necessitate other; it can also be how one experiences oneself in the world.

Asides from a few early poems in high school, I began writing more intensively in college and thereafter. It was around 1978 that I met the artist Mel Odom in New York via a mutually dear artist friend who said we reminded him of each other. While I could see a physical resemblance, more significantly I recognized something of myself in Mel's art. The way he rendered a face, a figure, capturing something immediate and sensual while also uncovering a more mysterious, archetypal aspect seemed to mirror my own romantic predisposition. Though our mutual friend, along with so many others, passed away during the height of the AIDS crisis, and despite our not seeing each other for years at a time, Mel and I always maintained that special connection, and all this time I hoped that his art might someday grace my own book.

Extending over six decades, the poems in this book comprise a kind of archaeological expedition, digging through histories of romantic feelings and reveries, trying to trace from whence they come, what they signify. In retrospect, it's not a question of how lasting or illusory these were. They are as genuine as figures excavated at Pompeii that might readily crumble, yet preserve an impression of their lived experience, of a moment, a world, all the more precious for being fleeting. Included as well are lyrics to two songs I wrote in the early days of my band Indoor Life and that relate to the overarching theme. The book truly is collaborative in that Mel Odom's drawings graciously complement the textual half, words and images juxtaposed that together they might dig deeper into the mysteries of Eros. It also represents a continuing collaboration with Josh Cheon and the Dark Entries imprint, without which this book might still just be a romantic fantasy.

JORGE SOCARRAS

INDEX OF POEMS

BRUCE

That first time we were alone together
I put my mouth to yours and asked,
What does this taste like to you?
And whatever unmemorable taste
had served as alibi
was quickly displaced
by something like berries and wood
and sundrenched air
distilling their dew in the night,
the taste that lingers still.

TRACES

. . . through waiting rooms,
   behind dressing tables,
  over aisles of footprints,
     under currents of dark smoke,
   where I last saw you
                     is where the searching began;
      my origin is in your traces . . .

POMPEII *(for Avram)*

It was there that the molten and ash found their embraces and
reaffirmed them.
It was there that each instance of tenderness became an icon in
the rich galleries:
the touch of a hand, neck, thigh, thus endowed with the duration
of stone.
And there also must be where I first dared pull you against me
in anticipation of a million cool nights strung together shadowless
and wise.
There is preserved the memory for my current flesh
—how it comes to me now like dust from the site
while you sit combing your hair with your fingers.
This time I do not hold you; I wed you with the ring of moon bronze
before the rain of ashes, before the flowering of ruins,
in the stillness of insects.
In a veil of glances remains the buried kiss.

TO THE EXTENT

To the extent that I can slip your face
over the contours of those who fill the streets
so I love you.
I will see an ancient man, perhaps a Hasidic,
and I will match your ear to his
so that it is you emerging from under wrinkles and white,
from *payis* and *shtreimel*,
the strength of your forearms is bared
under the rolled up sleeves of workmen everywhere,
the streets thrive with the possibility of you,
every dweller carrying a mystery as endearing,
passing your name from one to another
—a prayer I divine.
Only your frailty eludes comparison.
No one else will drape a coat over his shoulders
with such delicate sorrow.

½ of Christ

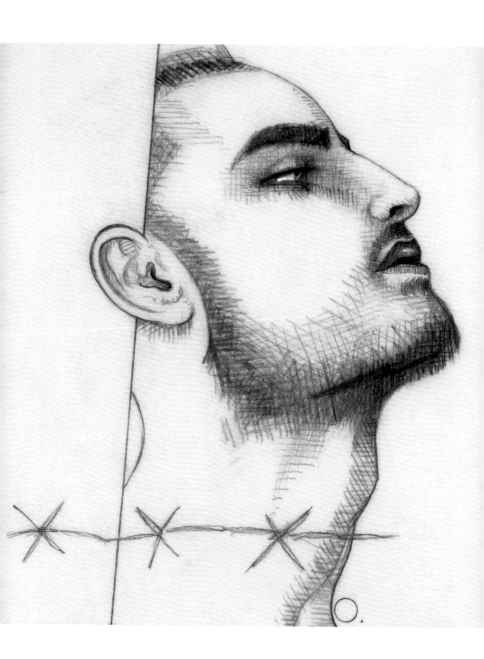

PINBALL FLASH

In a pinball flash I came to the signal of your beauty,
to your pulse irrevocable and forgotten in memorization,
Through corridors of smoke I came to the smiling corner where
you landed,
to the bridge of your nose, the space between your brows,
your shades darkening the designation,
Your cheeks, your jaw: a sharp mask for the laughter of recognition,
Your mouth an abandoned altar—not the end of my pilgrimage,
but its very confirmation.

THE CONFUSION OF DESIRE

In the confusion of desire
when any lover can unwittingly play messenger
    and deliver before me
        the stealthy warmth inside your knee
        or the Campari tint of your mouth
thus assembling the perfect absence of your body,
    so perhaps
        down an avenue of haberdashers
            will you recognize
        in the hollow of a stranger's back
some displaced splendor of mine.

THE MUMMY

You say you have never been
so despondent
You say you have never been
closer to death
You say you are so disillusioned
That those most meaningful to you
disillusion you most
You say I underestimate how much
I mean to you
You say I am your only friend
You say you are not listened to
You are not taken seriously
You say you are ready
to leave.

The mummy carried her deeper
and deeper into the swamp
He could not have her in this world
so he took her the only way he could
And she, in the stupor of the tana balm
ceased to resist
for now she gazed upon his soul.
With each step in his arms her young beauty
yielded to a deeper age.
Lines surfaced her face, her lips became white
Those who had pursued her rescue
remained aghast at the swamp's edge
unbeknown guests as the mummy and his bride
vanished 'neath the mist.

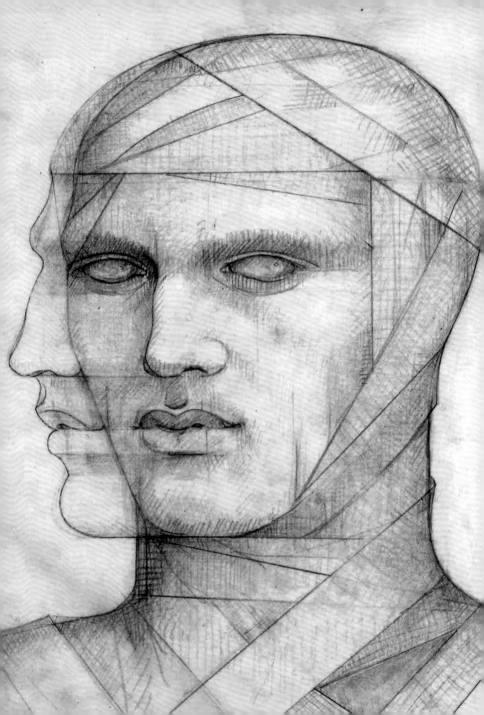

ROBIN

Ah, Robin
your beauty, the code of your histories
    every feature a glyph
                of your knowledge
your beauty, the perfection of your suffering
    the intelligence of your nature
    the indications of a permeating wisdom
in the alignment of your features
in the sway of your hips.
Your mouth,
        the passageway of discovery
        the shock enlightenment
                of touch
        the shortcut of the senses.

CONTRE NATURE

A thing of beauty, a work of art
So refined and so apart
Such a dandy, such a dilettante
A lofty mind and a wanton heart

Deliverer of my dreams
Seeker of my memories
Spectator of my tragedy
Perfect lover murdering

All my past and all my treasure
All my tastes against nature
My attacks of aphasia
I look back and see the future

Wake me from sleep, open the gate
Wrap me in sheets, walk me through flame
My pain to keep, my pleasure to take
Yours to free, yours to enslave

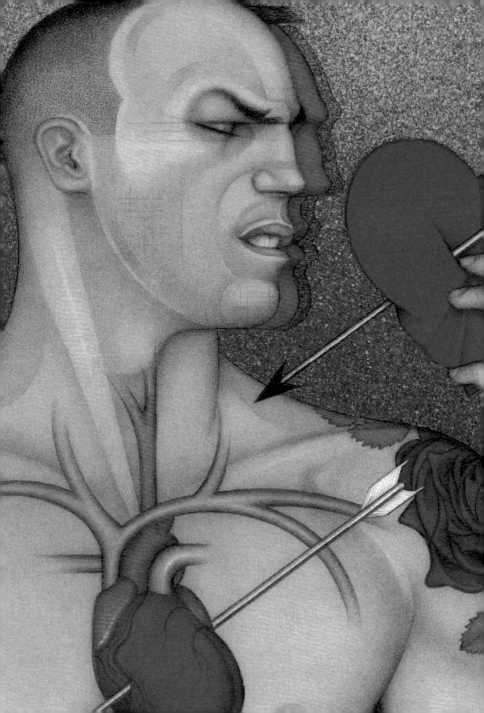

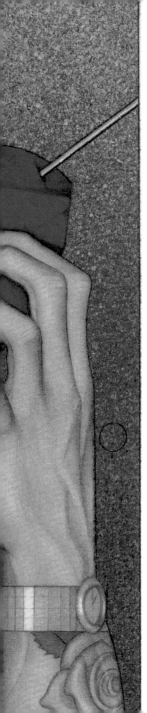

I HAVE SEEN YOU BEFORE

I have seen you before
in gatherings immemorial
In drunken crowds
that take strange drugs and music
to forget time
I have seen your face
immediate and preoccupied
I have seen it before
stretched over bone of some swift animal
a gazelle, elegantly stunned
the scent of destiny residing
in each nervous breath
those dark and upturned eyes
umbra of forests
of cities infringing
such black hair blown by a wind
from the Pyrenees
from the Levant
east from the source of your brow

And that neck so inclined I have seen before
delirium its ascent
its descent divine
from the imminent kiss
always suspended
on your warm tinted mouth
to your white limbs and spine and belly
that in languor grace
a divan I excavate
so many times

I have seen you there in tents and chambers
            in the pleasure of majesty
               and the spur of conquerors
            in the throes of knaves
              and priests confounded
            in the debauched communion
                 of painters and poets
   and rendered inaccessible
            in this time irreconcilable
                  you put forth your accounts
                  to remind the senses.

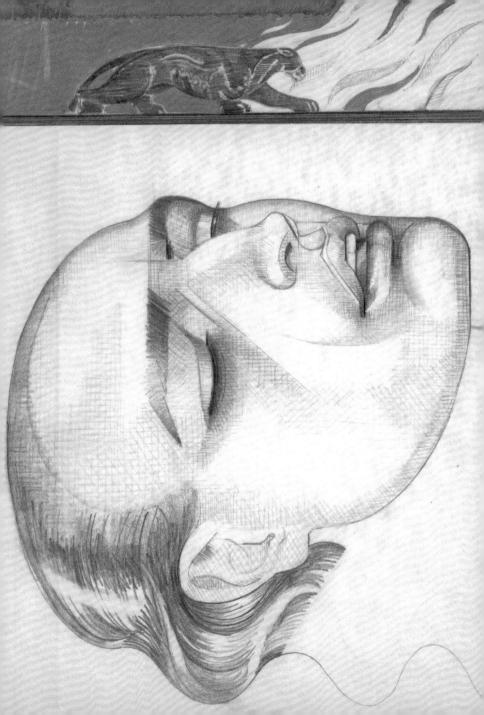

VERSAILLES

In those figures of Versailles
In those forms of snow and marble
I have sought the perfection
of fraternity immemorial
of hitchhikers in acid rains
and cloaked Arabs holding hands
of Chinese tagging by the shoulders
and Romans calling "Bello!"
but the splendor of men's greater days
is revealed succinct
in the sanctity of your tears
and the wisdom
               of your kiss.

BY THAT TOMB . . .

By that tomb, cool and still
as the gaze of gods
in relief against the stone
we kissed
and by this ardor stirred
a thousand scarabs, lapis and gold
their secret droned,
each treasure interred
to comfort the soul
its story told,
and all your splendor
in my arms
resounded life eternal.

MOVIE STAR

You crossed the room
your eyes everywhere
wondering who might recognize you
—leather-bounded elegance

You crossed in front of me
and I searched for the gesture
penetrative enough
to let you know indeed and more

In a movie you had come to me
removed as a ghost
stirring up memories invented
to accommodate you
like all the other seats
of veneration

But I saw you look at me
I saw your eyes wondering
why I was looking at you
both of us bound and helpless

THE MINOTAUR'S VALENTINE

Sprung from the brow of a restless god
      hurled into a quest unknown
through a labyrinth of bloodstained walls
      that some forgotten dream recalls

The listless face of an alabaster saint
      calling fools to pray and weep
eyes colored by a distant harbor
      an angel's mouth that bespeaks ardor

All about the terrible child
      passions like many serpents coil
ghosts that feast on flesh abound
      a horned shadow hunts him down

Driven by the buried vision
      maddened by his legacy
running from the thing he seeks
      fighting what he cannot see

Beyond the promise of his manhood
      from the heart his own hand pierced
over hooved prints his own feet led
      torrents of roses flowing red.

DANIEL

black angels hovering
over a yellow taxi
paved earth cradling
lovers in the back seat
radio shepherds sing
night kisses morning

DENE *(after Rumi)*

I went east along timeless rivers
  where morning mists rise over golden temples
    and dark throngs dip
      that they be blessed
But in the warmth of your gaze
  your smiling grace
    I felt content

I went out into empty deserts
  where phantom winds rise over fiery dunes
    and nomads seek
      that they be quenched
But in the stream of your voice
  your laughter's flow
    was I refreshed

I went up over ruined cities
  which once did rise over teeming streets
    and wise men reigned
      and lovers dreamed
Still in your dusky beauty
  carelessly bestowed
    all is perfection

THIS DAY

this day   of boundless light newly made

this day   no other can surpass and all others take their splendor from

this day   river and breeze   ray of sun   branch of tree
             all play along while we   laughing glide   quiet lie
             the earth beneath our bodies
                             thoughts rising to the sky
            warmth and happiness   indistinguishable
       the essence of it all condensed   in a drop upon your neck
     a taste of salt I steal away   that I might live again
this day

THE KISS

I imbibed of your kiss just before sleep
and fell quite drunk unfathomably deep
through layers of faces that sloughed off like skins
and myriad souls that mingled in dream
'til from the source of it all waiting within
the day arose that I might kiss you again.

THE ARCHAEOLOGY OF EROS

I EXCAVATE THE LAYERS OF YOU
BECAUSE THEY ARE A PART OF ME
AND THUS BIT BY BIT WE DISAPPEAR
UNTIL ALL THAT REMAINS
       IS AN EMBRACE
             OF MELDED BONE
             AND UNDYING FLAME

IN A ROOM

In a room of quiet splendor
with a view to sky and see
a room of vision rendered
in a manner painterly
where glass and wood and textile
light and color blend
and the painter's daily rituals
living vibrance lend

In a room furnished with treasures
of heartfelt luxury
with portraits and with relics
from the halls of memory
with icons and depictions
of what cannot be seen
of quest and myth and fiction
eternal mysteries
where waves of moonlight glisten
over golden limbs in sleep
to be ever reflected
in eyes so blue and deep

and when the soul surrenders
to flights of whim and dream
in a room of quiet splendor
how heavenly you seem

HARSHA

I pondered the grace of deity
in luxuriant curves, serpentine spine
from whose coils emerge all worlds and time
poised in embrace with consort divine

I recited the verse of saints who imbibe
intoxicant tropes, sphinxian lines,
from whose coils emerge paradoxical rhymes
invoking a trace of presence divine

Then hearing your voice the artisan cried
drenched in the sweat of a mythmaking night
a cry that stirs lovers moonlit and wise
and touching your neck the poet resigned
to marvel at passions that unfurling rise
beyond reach of words save for two names
                              in one breath entwined

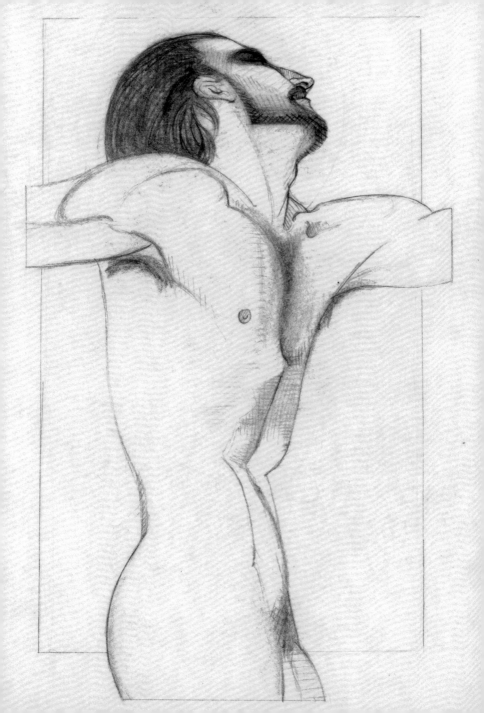

SLOWLY

Slowly as budding bits of green
I watch you become real
can almost touch you
your waist, neck, your mouth
nearly materialized before me
your quickening breath, gasps of pleasure
as I invoke your name

Slowly as I come to know you
you grow less fantastic
and more the man I need
image giving way to heart
the one I dreamed of
my dream displacing
your voice reassuring
there is life to come
a world of our making
where we begin each day
where we fend for our joy
slowly growing
slowly transforming
slowly, baby, slowly . . .

GOOD FRIDAY

On this day of sunny gloom
ancient rites of death and rebirth
disguised for those who cannot see
I contemplate the wonder of you

How fitting that we met at an airport
flying towards eternal sunset
me resigned to the finality of my pilgrimage
you ascending, wings outspread

I tell you now these things
talismans for your safe keep:
you are the perfection of all I've sought
template for all my hypothetical loves
All those gardens of ruined statues
visions of ancient poets and seers
stir and come to life again in you
laugh and dance and moan and sigh

How I lose myself in your sleepy head!
You close your eyes and it is I who dream
running my fingers along each bit of you
painting you in my memory
the vision I will carry always
the final evidence that life is worthwhile
the redemption of man unkind
the glory of spirit divine

FILE THIS

Take this memory and file it,
This image of you reclined
like Adonis come to earth
adored in all your glory
touched by heavenly light
somewhere outside time
where you remain suspended
your foot rising to meet a starry kiss
moans escaping like small birds from your rustling limbs;
know that you were loved with passion unbridled,
that you were the elixir one mortal sought
who drank deep—too deep it seems
and left behind this vision
of wonder for you.
Know that this moment is yours always
a jewel for you to ponder
when the world seems dim
and men even dimmer;
know that you were loved
as few have been.

File this away then
that you may wonder at it all anew.

HOMAGE VIA FRANK O'HARA

All the mornings I lay awake while you slept,
Our arms entwined, our dreams perhaps not,
Taking stock of every blessing before me,
Your every freckle, every breath, every lovely line,
Not wanting to sleep through any of it,
Knowing that this was life's most joyous moment,
Knowing the gods could not be so generous forever,
Knowing that I could never finish these lovely lines
more elegantly than your best-loved poet,
"O you were the best of all my days."*

*Quote from "Animals" by Frank O'Hara, 1950

HOW MANY NIGHTS?

How many nights I must have just missed
Seeing you across that proverbial crowded room,
How many times might we have kissed
Had not the gods deemed it too soon

How many lovers I might have spared
My fickle pleasure, my dissatisfied gloom,
Searching, not finding—each one reminding
That what I was seeking was yet far removed

How many years I watched and waited
Reading the signs, all phases of moon,
By passion kept blinded, by hope kept elated
What gypsy divined, what sage could construe
The face in the dream that carried me through
The seasons, the stations, the vicissitudes
The quixotic romances I kept staging anew
So when at last I found you I'd not miss my cue?

STEVE

When was it that we walked out on the sand
and hand in hand left the world afar,
that our lips met and searched for ways
to say those things that can't be said
while the night stood guard all around,
stars trembling to the ocean's sound
and a wind fragrant with earth's mystery
conveyed to us the history
of lovers who had stood before
braced against time's mortal shore?

When was it you lay close to me
in my vagrant arms asleep
and as your dreamy head I stroked
my own contented coos invoked,
and with each breath drank you in
as if my soul had found its skin?

FACEBOOK ADONIS

While leafing through the book of faces,
at many posts from many places
I chanced upon a photograph that seemed to have been cropped in half
A young man stretched upon the floor like Adonis poised to be adored
with torso bare and skin so fair, and dark storm o'er his head for hair
and bearded chin that barely hid the boyishness of his satyr grin
His nipples like twin Saturns shone,
beckoning "touch and make me moan"
while finely streaking hairs between like comet tails the heavens glean
This then would my pleasure be, to have this lad lay close to me
For this one wish I'd make him feel a god descended here to steal
a night of mortal bliss with man, that he might come to understand
e'er his beauty and his grace reside far above the sin of pride
and what inspiration poets know is his privilege to bestow.
Oh to trace the lovely lines of that arm heavenly inclined
and exalt him that he might recall how once he soared above us all!

NICLAS

Walking in the wake of your company
the joys of night welling up all around
the moon half delirious creaming down
on lovers kissing in the street
by a storefront where a psychic reads
palms seeking out a destiny
while I just smile contentedly
rapt in the perfection of everything
our words and warmth lingering still
in the summer evening breeze
and hours that we shared soon fill
a darkened cinema with dreams.

SCORPIO MOON

Under the Scorpio moon I wonder
under the Scorpio moon I dream
under the fullness of things invisible
under the spell of loves unlived

Long, long ago you ruled me
compelled me towards your mystery
in each new face resurrecting
this deep atavistic need

To find you again in that night
where the light reaches us finally
and messages older than time
resound in the depth of our being

Here then, here now I call you
hear how the earth starts to sing
falling in blissful oblivion
spinning in ecstatic rings

Under the Scorpio moon I wander
through memories and futures unseen
seeking that which was sundered
and still looms luminous o'er me.

STRANGER

A face appeared and I wondered
Who might this handsome stranger be?
His gaze intense and yet familiar
Looking out so fervently

A voice spoke and I responded
Its dark warmth at once touching me
As with a long-lost friend forgotten
We traced converging histories

And when his face lay close to mine
Our arms encircling in bliss
My fears and hurts and doubts resigned
As wordlessly I brushed his lips

Now the stranger disappears
I'm spellbound by his sorcery
For though I long to feel him near
It is his burning heart I see.

THERE WAS NO MISTLETOE

Was it your voice I saw?
Was it your face I heard?
Was it something in me?
Some unspoken words
that flew to you
like hummingbirds
to their flowering home
to drink in the nectar
that so freely flowed
imbibe of your laughter
the warmth of your soul

Was it your gesture?
Your finger to cheek
offering the pleasure
for my lips to seek
that something unexpected
prompted in me

There was no mistletoe
There was no need
The magic was conjured
The ritual complete
The mystery made flesh
The kiss takes wing.

EN UN JARDÍN

Ese brillante primer día me mostraste un jardín
refugio de un príncipe donde hace siglos
contempló los secretos de su corazón,
y aunque era verde, no se veían flores
porque era invierno en Madrid.
Entonces, sin nadie más alrededor, te besé
y en ese jardín aún más escondido pude saborear
una primavera por venir
y la calidez de un príncipe conmovedor.

FIRST POEM *(after e. e. cummings)*

photographs of sunsets
               can't warm this room
the ceiling is like the January sky
but your smile—actual sunrise—melts the snow
April sings prayers for the dead—victims of the blizzard of '88
March came but a row of days
                         ahead . . .
        more sunlight
            basking on the beach
        fun takes many forms
        I love your form
        let's go for a swim

ARCHAEOLOGY

They will know who I am
They will recognize me
They will make out my name
by a mark on the street
when the cities fall
here we will remain
embedded in cement
with only signs to explain
the fated behemoth
the man who tames the beast
will not lie forgotten
ever old, ever deep,
and dig and dig and dig
the future waits beneath
until they excavate
until they set us free . . .

We will meet again!

JORGE SOCARRAS

Born and raised in New York City, Jorge Socarras studied fine art at the SVA before moving to San Francisco in 1971. There he pursued creative arts at SFSU and met musician-composer Patrick Cowley, forming the duo Catholic. He also started writing poetry and fiction. In 1980 Jorge formed the avant-rock band Indoor Life, over the next seven years touring and recording to critical acclaim. When not touring he worked as doorman at New York's most legendary clubs. In 1987, responding to the AIDS crisis, Jorge took a hiatus from music and cofounded the Silence=Death Collective, together designing the iconic poster and slogan. After completing a first novel manuscript, he returned to SFSU and obtained an M.A. in Humanities. He then taught writing at Rutgers, worked as copywriter in the New York art world, and completed a second novel, *The Immortal's Last Breath*, published independently. The 2009 release of the original Catholic recordings and successive reissue of Indoor Life's discography rebooted Jorge's music career, embarking him on new collaborations, notably with Mathias Schaffhäuser as Fanatico X. In 2019 together with Dark Entries he published Patrick Cowley's erotic diary, and finally at age 70 thought it was time to publish his own poems. Now living in Madrid, Jorge is writing a novel about coming of age in New York during the summer of love.

MEL ODOM

Mel Odom first attained artistic prominence in the mid-1970s with a series of erotic illustrations done for magazines such as *Blueboy* and *VIVA*. These pencil and watercolor drawings soon attracted assignments from art directors higher up the publishing chain, including a seventeen-year, freelance relationship with *Playboy* magazine, and covers for *Time* and *Omni* magazines as well as countless books. Along with a line of cards and posters, Mel's art has been the subject of two books of drawings published in America and Japan. Post illustration career, he created a sophisticated fashion doll for adults named Gene Marshall, voted the most influential doll since Barbie. After twenty years of being a "doll mogul" Mel returned to two-dimensional art and resumed painting and drawing. His one-man show at New York's Daniel Cooney Fine Art Gallery in 2019 was a smash. Featuring an in-gallery "conversation" between Mel and author Edmund White, the show was given a rave review in *ARTFORUM* magazine. Mel lives in New York City and continues to create art.

ART CREDITS

DARK ENTRIES
E D I T I O N S

www.darkentriesrecords.com